BRUCE & STAN'S®

POCK

D0834767

Knowing The Holy Spirit

BRUCE BICKEL and STAN JANTZ

HARVEST HOUSE PUBLISHERS
Eugene, Oregon 97402

Cover design by Left Coast Design, Portland, Oregon

Cover illustration by Krieg Barrie Illustrations, Hoquiam, Washington

BRUCE & STAN'S® POCKET GUIDE TO KNOWING THE HOLY SPIRIT
Copyright © 2002 by Bruce Bickel and Stan Jantz
Published by Harvest House Publishers
Eugene, Oregon 97402

Bickel, Bruce, 1952–
   Bruce & Stan's pocket guide to the Holy Spirit / Bruce Bickel and Stan Jantz.
     p. cm.
  ISBN 0-7369-0645-2
     1. Holy Spirit.   2. Theology, Doctrinal—Popular works.   I. Title: Bruce and Stan's pocket guide to the Holy Spirit.   II. Title: Pocket guide to the Holy Spirit.   III. Jantz, Stan, 1952–   IV. Title.
BT121.3B53 2002
231'.3—dc21   2001038502

Printed in the United States of America

02 03 04 05 06 07 08 09 / BP-CF / 10 9 8 7 6 5 4 3 2 1

Contents

A Note from the Authors

"May the Force be with you" is one of the most famous lines in movie history. It also may be one of the dumbest. What is the "Force" anyway? Is it a predictable power, like gravity? Or is it some kind of mysterious energy, like the wind? Either way, a force is impersonal and can't be *with* anybody—unless you walk with the wind at your back or you plant your head beneath a falling object (in which case the force is not *with* you as much as it is *on* you).

The concept of force isn't limited to the world of movies, physics, and nature. A lot of people apply it to their belief system as well. When they hear the word *spiritual* or *Spirit,* they think about a force that appears in the form of a ghost, a vapor trail, or something discussed on *Oprah.* And when they hear someone talk about the Holy Spirit, well, then their imaginations run wild.

What comes to your mind when you think about the Holy Spirit? Do you think the Holy Spirit is something that—

- Makes people talk in strange "tongues" that sound a lot like someone is trying to make up a language;

- Causes other people to fall back and roll around on the floor;

- Gets tossed around the stage of a civic auditorium by some guy with a bad comb over; or

- Is irrelevant to any thinking Christian because it is all about emotions?

Let's face it. There are a lot of misconceptions about the Holy Spirit, even among Christians. That's why we wrote this pocket guide. We want to help you know the truth about who the Holy Spirit is and what He does, because He can either become very real to you and make a huge difference in your life, or He can continue to be a mysterious stranger who means nothing to you. It all depends on how well you know the Holy Spirit.

Why You Should Know the Holy Spirit

The Holy Spirit may not be as popular as God (who is the object of worship for billions of people) or as tangible as Jesus (who walked the earth as God in the flesh), but He is just as real and just as important. That's why you need to know that—

- ✓ The Holy Spirit is a person and not a force.

- ✓ The Holy Spirit is the key to knowing God better.

- ✓ The Holy Spirit helps you understand the Word of God more clearly.

- ✓ The Holy Spirit can enable you to become more effective in your faith.

- ✓ The Holy Spirit has given you some unique gifts that will energize your life.

How to Use This Book

We have designed this pocket guide so you can read it straight through in one or two sittings (depending on how long you can sit). To help you navigate through the various topics, we have inserted some icons along the way so you can pause and go "hmmm" from time to time (it helps to stroke your chin in a thoughtful manner when you do this).

Big Idea—This icon saves you the trouble of marking the sentence with a yellow highlighter. It's that important.

Key Verse—Every verse from the Bible is significant, but this icon identifies the ones that are worth rereading before you move on down the page.

It's a Mystery—We don't know everything about the Holy Spirit, but then again, nobody does. At least we admit it.

Glad You Asked—You aren't alone when it comes to wondering about the Holy Spirit. We can anticipate some of your questions because we've asked them ourselves.

Learn the Lingo—We try to stay away from terminology that you might hear from people who try to impress you with how smart they are. We aren't that smart, but from time to time we use words that need an explanation.

Dig Deeper—This book is just a pocket guide to the subject of the Holy Spirit. We encourage you to study further, and we suggest some of the books that helped us better understand this fascinating subject.

A Final Word Before You Start

Before you read any book, it's important to establish the author's (or in our case, the authors') point of view. This helps you better interpret and understand what the book is trying to say. So before you dive into this book, we want to give you our point of view on the Holy Spirit.

We believe the Holy Spirit is a real person rather than a spiritual force for one very simple reason. As Dr. James Boice points out, if you think the Holy Spirit is a force or a power, then you will always want to know, "How can I get more of the Holy Spirit?" But if you think of the Holy Spirit as a real person, then you will want to know, "How can the Holy Spirit have more of me?" Our prayer for you is that by the time you are finished with this book, you will want the Holy Spirit to have more of you.

CHAPTER 1

JUST WHO IS THE HOLY SPIRIT ANYWAY?

> *If the Holy Spirit is a divine Person,
> worthy to receive our adoration, our faith,
> and our love, and we do not know and
> recognize him as such, then we are rob-
> bing a divine Being of the adoration and
> love and confidence which are his due.*
>
> —R. A. Torrey

As a couple of guys, we have this natural craving for more power. Like Tim "the Tool Man" Taylor on TV's "Home Improvement," we want more power in everything from our cars to our computers. A lot of Christians see the Holy Spirit as some kind of power tool that exists just so they can turbocharge their spiritual lives.

We want to be very clear right here in the first chapter that this is a huge misconception. Yes, the Holy Spirit is powerful, and God wants you to have more power through the Holy Spirit, but it's not going to happen in the ways you might think. Later in the book you're going to find out how the Holy Spirit works. But first you need to discover who the Holy Spirit is.

Bruce & Stan

Chapter 1

Just Who Is the Holy Spirit Anyway?

*A*re you hooked on spiritual steroids? Are you addicted to performance-enhancing Christian activities or gimmicks so you can gain confidence and feel adequate when it comes to living your Christian life? If you're not sure, here's a little test:

- Do you want to be a super-Christian, but you feel more like a Clark Kent Christian?

- Do you go to church three times a week and sign up for every retreat, seminar, and weekend spiritual experience you can find?

- Do you watch TV evangelists and listen to radio preachers?

- Have you read the latest Christian book offering "Five Easy Ways to Supersize Your Spiritual Life"?

- Have you ever attended one of those giant rallies where some guy in a white suit promises to give you a substantial portion of the Holy Spirit's power (as long as you give him a substantial portion of the contents of your wallet)?

If you answered "yes" to all five questions, then you are probably addicted to spiritual steroids and in need of immediate help (for immediate help, keep reading). If you answered "yes" to all but the last question, then you are probably not in any danger. In fact, you need to be doing things like going to church, attending special seminars now and then, and reading books that help you grow as a Christian (especially books by Bruce & Stan).

What you have to watch for—and this can happen to the best of us—is becoming so focused on adding outside spiritual activities to your life that you neglect your inner spiritual growth. To put it another way:

Never substitute the work of people on the outside for the work of God on the inside.

What Is True Spirituality?

The reason people try so hard to add spiritual activities to their lives is that they want to be spiritual. There's nothing wrong with that. God wants you to be spiritual, which is another way of saying that He wants you to see everything and do everything from His perspective. That's because "God is Spirit, so those who worship him must worship in spirit and in truth" (John 4:24).

Becoming a truly spiritual person is impossible to do on your own. You need help. That's where the Holy Spirit comes in. The Holy Spirit's job is to help you become spiritually minded in everything you do so that two things will happen:

- You will see the world from God's perspective.

- The world will see God's perspective in you.

What the Holy Spirit Isn't

The Holy Spirit is not an activity you can add to your life. The Holy Spirit is not a thing you can acquire or a commodity you can buy. There's nothing you can do to earn the Holy Spirit. The spiritual power and confidence you are looking for aren't available in church or in a special TV offer. The Holy Spirit isn't a force, an influence, or Jamba Juice power boost. The Holy Spirit is a divine Person. The Holy Spirit is God. Just like you don't use God, you don't use the Holy Spirit. The Holy Spirit uses you.

There are many misconceptions about who the Holy Spirit is and how He works. That's why we need to go to the Bible and find out the truth about the Holy Spirit.

The Holy Spirit Is a Person

The first thing you need to know is that the Holy Spirit is a Person. This is a very big deal. If the Holy Spirit is not a Person, then He can't be God, because in addition to being a Spirit, God is a Person. And if the Holy Spirit isn't God, then He can't do the things the Bible says He can do. So how do we know the Holy Spirit is a Person?

The Holy Spirit Has Qualities Only a Person Can Have

- The Holy Spirit has *intellect.* He searches out everything (1 Corinthians 2:10).

- The Holy Spirit has *knowledge,* especially knowledge about God (1 Corinthians 2:11).

- The Holy Spirit has *emotions,* such as sorrow (Ephesians 4:30).

- The Holy Spirit has a *will* that can make decisions (Acts 16:6).

- The Holy Spirit *loves* (Romans 15:30).

A force or an influence can't think or feel or will something. Only a person can do these things. Clearly, the Holy Spirit is a Person.

The Holy Spirit Does Things Only a Person Would Do

Another reason we know that the Holy Spirit is a person and not just a force or influence is that He does things a force couldn't possibly do:

- The Holy Spirit *teaches* you things about God and you (John 14:26).

- The Holy Spirit *tells the truth,* especially the truth about Jesus (John 15:26).

- The Holy Spirit *guides* you (John 16:13).

- The Holy Spirit *convinces* you that you need God (John 16:8).

- The Holy Spirit *prays* for you (Romans 8:26,27).

- The Holy Spirit *commands* you to do things (Acts 13:2).

THINGS YOU CAN DO TO THE HOLY SPIRIT

Like God, the Holy Spirit is a perfect gentleman. He won't force Himself on you (like gravity or that sinking feeling you get after eating bad chili). As you will see in chapter 2, you have to invite the Holy Spirit into your life through Jesus, and then you must make the daily decision to let the Holy Spirit fill your life. Even though the Holy Spirit will never force Himself on you, it is possible for you to resist the Holy Spirit (Acts 7:51). You can also bring sorrow to the Holy Spirit (Ephesians 4:30), and you can lie to the Holy Spirit (Acts 5:3). Of course, you also have the option to obey the Holy Spirit (Acts 16:6), which is by far the best thing you can do.

The Holy Spirit Is God

We have mentioned a couple of times that the Holy Spirit is God. We need to explain why this is important and why this is true.

Why It's Important That the Holy Spirit Is God

Here is one of the most important verses in the Bible about you and the Holy Spirit:

Or don't you know that your body is the temple of the Holy Spirit, who lives in you and was given to you by God? (1 Corinthians 6:19).

When you invite God to come into your life by believing in Jesus Christ, it's the Holy Spirit who literally moves into you and lives in your body. This isn't some force or feeling. It's God Himself—in you! The Holy Spirit makes your personal, intimate, immediate relationship with God possible. If the Holy Spirit isn't God, then you don't have such a relationship with God.

Why It's True That the Holy Spirit Is God

The most compelling reason we know that the Holy Spirit is God is that the Holy Spirit has characteristics that only God has:

- The Holy Spirit is *all-knowing* (omniscient).

  But we know these things because God has revealed them to us by his Spirit, and his Spirit searches out everything and shows us even God's deep secrets (1 Corinthians 2:10).

- The Holy Spirit is *all-powerful* (omnipotent).

  The angel replied, "The Holy Spirit will come upon you, and the power of the Most High will overshadow you. So the baby born to you will be holy, and he will be called the Son of God" (Luke 1:35).

- The Holy Spirit is *everywhere at once* (omnipresent).

  I can never escape from your spirit! I can never get away from your presence! (Psalm 139:7).

- The Holy Spirit is *eternal.*

  For by the power of the eternal Spirit, Christ offered himself to God as a perfect sacrifice for our sins (Hebrews 9:14).

- The Holy Spirit is *equal to God.*

Then Peter said, "Ananias, why has Satan filled your heart? You lied to the Holy Spirit, and you kept some of the money for yourself....How could you do a thing like this? You weren't lying to us but to God" (Acts 5:3,4).

THE HOLY SPIRIT AND THE TRINITY

The Holy Spirit is a living being and a divine Person. He is equal to God and one of the three Persons of the Trinity. The concept of the Trinity is one of the most mysterious and difficult things you will ever encounter as a Christian. Here is our definition from *Bruce & Stan's Guide to God*—

> Essentially the Trinity describes the three distinct Persons of God, which make up the one true God: God the Father, God the Son, and God the Holy Spirit.

Trinity does not mean there are three gods who together make up God. That would be *tritheism.* God is one (Deuteronomy 6:4). Instead, the concept of the Trinity describes what theologians call the "fullness of the Godhead," including God's unity and His diversity. This essentially defines the *tri-unity* of God. There is only one God, but within that unity are three eternal and co-equal Persons—all sharing the same essence and substance, but each having a distinct existence.

If you don't quite get this difficult concept, you're in good company. We aren't very good at explaining it, and even Billy Graham writes, "I have never fully resolved it, for it contains an aspect of mystery." To complicate matters more, the word *trinity* doesn't even appear in the Bible. But the evidence for the Trinity is clearly there.

Mark 1:9-11—When Jesus was baptized by John in the Jordan River, God the Father spoke from heaven as the Holy Spirit came upon Jesus in the form of a dove.

Matthew 28:19—The last words of Jesus on earth included these: "Therefore, go and make disciples of all the nations, baptizing them in the name of the Father and the Son and the Holy Spirit."

2 Corinthians 13:13—The apostle Paul wrote, "May the grace of our Lord Jesus Christ, the love of God, and the fellowship of the Holy Spirit be with you all."

The Bible clearly teaches that the Holy Spirit is one with the Father and one with the Son.

The Holy Spirit in History

 One of the most dramatic days in the history of the world occurred about 2000 years ago in Jerusalem. Called the Day of Pentecost, this was when the Holy Spirit came upon the believers, empowering them to spread the good news about Jesus throughout the world (Acts 2:1-4). We're going to talk more about this in chapter 2, but for now we've got to answer a question you are probably asking: What was the Holy Spirit doing before He came upon the believers on the Day of Pentecost?

Because He is God, the Holy Spirit has always existed. So where was He before New Testament times? Was He kicking back while God and Jesus did all the work? Hardly. As we're going to show you, the Holy Spirit was there every step of the way. He wasn't involved in the everyday lives of believers like He has been since Pentecost, but the Holy Spirit has been active in every important part of history, starting at the beginning.

The Holy Spirit and Creation

The first verse of the Bible is also the most important:

In the beginning God created the heavens and the earth (Genesis 1:1).

Without Creation, there's no universe. Without the universe, there are no people—and that includes you! But did God act alone in this supernatural and supremely powerful creative process, or were all three members of the Trinity involved? The first clue is in the first verse. The Hebrew word for "God" in Genesis 1:1 is *Elohim,* which is in the plural form rather than the singular. This means that all the Persons of the Godhead—Father, Son, and Holy Spirit—were present and involved in Creation. (Also see Genesis 1:2.)

This plurality pops up again when God created humans in His image: "Let us make people in our image" (Genesis 1:26). In the New Testament the apostle Paul made it clear that Jesus was involved in Creation (Colossians 1:16), and in the Old Testament Job understood this about the Holy Spirit's role in creation:

> *For the Spirit of God has made me, and the breath of the Almighty gives me life* (Job 33:4).

The Holy Spirit and Inspiration

Without the Holy Spirit, we wouldn't have the Bible. It's as simple as that. As we explain in *Bruce & Stan's Guide to the Bible*, God "wrote" the Scriptures by inspiring 40 different human authors to write down His words over a period of nearly 2000 years. The word *inspiration* literally means to "breathe in," and the way God "breathed in" was through the Holy Spirit. Here's how the Bible explains it:

Above all, you must understand that no prophecy in Scripture ever came from the prophets themselves or because they wanted to prophesy. It was the Holy Spirit who moved the prophets to speak from God (2 Peter 1:20,21).

The Holy Spirit and New Life

In the New Testament the apostle Paul explains what happens when you accept Jesus as your Savior:

What this means is that those who become Christians become new persons. They are not the same anymore, for the old life is gone. A new life has begun! (2 Corinthians 5:17).

The way you get this "new life" is through the Holy Spirit. Jesus explained this in a conversation with Nicodemus, who asked Jesus what it meant to be "born again":

> *Humans can reproduce only human life, but the Holy Spirit gives new life from heaven* (John 3:6).

This work of the Holy Spirit didn't start in the New Testament. The Holy Spirit was actively giving new life to people in the Old Testament as well. God told the prophet Ezekiel to give the nation of Israel this message: "I will give you a new heart with new and right desires, and I will put a new spirit in you" (Ezekiel 36:26).

The Breath of God
The Holy Spirit has sometimes been called the breath of God, and there are at least two instances where this image shows us how the Holy Spirit was involved in what God was doing.

Creation—Psalm 33:6 says that God "breathed the word, and all the stars were born." When God created humankind, He "breathed into it the breath of life" (Genesis 2:7).

Inspiration—In 2 Timothy 3:16 we read that all Scripture "is inspired by God." In other words, it is God-breathed.

The Holy Spirit and Indwelling

It has always been the Holy Spirit's job to indwell—or occupy—believers. But the way that indwelling works changed on the Day of Pentecost. Theologian Paul Enns explains that before Pentecost, the indwelling of the Holy Spirit was *selective* and *temporary.* The Holy Spirit indwelt Joshua (Numbers 27:18) and David (1 Samuel 16:12,13). In other cases the Holy Spirit came upon Gideon (Judges 6:34) and Samson (Judges 15:14,15), enabling them to win great battles.

After Pentecost, the indwelling of the Holy Spirit became a *permanent* part of the believer's life. Jesus promised this when He told His disciples:

And I will ask the Father, and he will give you another Counselor, who will never leave you. He is the Holy Spirit, who leads into all truth (John 14:16,17).

The Holy Spirit and the Restraint of Sin

Most of us worry that crime is out of control, but we should really be thankful that it's not worse. And the One we should thank is the Holy Spirit, who has always been in the business of restraining sin. "But there's so much sin!" you might reply. "The Holy Spirit needs to do a better job of restraining."

In fact, there is more crime (and more sin) because there are more people. An expert in criminology once told us that anywhere from one to two percent of the population is in jail or prison at any given time, and that number has remained constant over the years. So the truth is that *something* is keeping the percentage from getting higher, and that something is the Holy Spirit. We know this from verses in both the Old and New Testaments.

Genesis 6:3 tells us that the Holy Spirit was restraining sin, but would not put up with humanity's disobedience forever. He didn't, and the Great Flood wiped out all of humanity except for Noah and his family. And 2 Thessalonians 2:7,8 tells us that the Holy Spirit is holding back "lawlessness." That's the good news. The bad news is that someday the Holy Spirit will step out of the way. His restraint will be pulled off, and humanity will do what comes naturally—all the time. Bible scholars believe that when this happens, the Tribulation will begin (for more on this, see *Bruce & Stan's Guide to Bible Prophecy*).

The Holy Spirit and Jesus

There was no more important role for the Holy Spirit than in the life of Jesus. Isaiah prophesied that the Spirit would rest upon the Messiah and give Him wisdom, understanding, power, and knowledge (Isaiah 11:2). And He did. Jesus had all of these qualities already (because Jesus is God), but He chose to depend on the Holy Spirit and obey Him (Isaiah 11:3). Here are several ways that the Holy Spirit worked in Jesus.

- **The Virgin Birth**
  This inconceivable miracle of God taking human form and being born of a woman was made possible by the Holy Spirit (Matthew 1:20).

- **The Life and Ministry of Jesus**
  The Holy Spirit filled Jesus and directed Him (Luke 4:1), and then He anointed Jesus to preach the Good News (Luke 4:18).

- **The Death of Jesus**
  Not only was the Holy Spirit responsible for the birth of Jesus, but He also played a part in the death of Jesus. The Holy Spirit didn't put Jesus to

death, but He gave Jesus the power to offer Himself to God "as a perfect sacrifice for our sins" (Hebrews 9:14).

- **The Resurrection of Jesus**
  Each member of the Godhead played a part in the resurrection of Jesus. God the Father raised Jesus from the dead (Ephesians 1:19,20), but Jesus also had the power to raise Himself from the dead (John 10:18). And Romans 1:4 states that God raised Jesus from the dead "by means of the Holy Spirit."

The Holy Spirit, Jesus, and You

Since He is God, the Holy Spirit does everything that the Father and Son do. We've made that pretty clear. But there is one area where the Holy Spirit really shines (and we mean this in a literal sense). Jesus said it best:

> **Something to Think About**
> If Jesus, the Son of God, depended on the Holy Spirit, who are we to think we can live our lives with God without doing the same?

But I will send you the Counselor—the Spirit of truth. He will come to you from the Father and will tell you all about me (John 15:26).

He will bring me glory by revealing to you whatever he receives from me (John 16:14).

Do you see what Jesus is saying about the Holy Spirit? Allow us to summarize:

The primary work of the Holy Spirit is to tell us about Jesus and glorify Him.

To glorify means to praise, honor, and magnify. The Holy Spirit does this to Jesus. He directs our attention to Jesus. It's as if He is shining a giant spotlight on Jesus and saying, "Here He is, Jesus Christ. Above Him there is no other. Jesus is the way, the truth, and the life."

So what does this mean to you? It means that you need to see the Holy Spirit for who He is. The Holy Spirit isn't a force or a power tool for you to use. He is the one who gives you the desire and the ability to look at Jesus. As important as the Holy Spirit is, He should never take the place of Jesus in your mind or your heart. Be thankful that the light of the Holy Spirit will fill your life, but understand that the light is shining on Jesus.

> *The Holy Spirit is the celestial matchmaker who pairs us with Christ.*
>
> —J. I. Packer

"What's That Again?"

1. The only way to be truly spiritual is to allow the Holy Spirit to help you become spiritually minded in everything you do.

2. The Holy Spirit is not an activity, a force, or an influence that you can add to your life and use. The Holy Spirit is a divine Person who uses you.

3. The reason we know the Holy Spirit is a Person is that He has the qualities of a person and does the things a person does.

4. The reason we know the Holy Spirit is God is that He has characteristics only God has.

5. The Holy Spirit didn't first show up on the Day of Pentecost. He has been involved in the history of the world and in the lives of people from the very beginning.

6. The primary work of the Holy Spirit is to tell us about Jesus and glorify Him.

Dig Deeper

There are many good books about the Holy Spirit (and we hope we've added one more). Here are two others we think you will enjoy, along with a book of theology (theology is the study of God) that's written in an understandable style (believe us, not all books of theology are).

If you were going to read only one other book about the Holy Spirit, we would recommend *The Holy Spirit* by Billy Graham. His illustrations are wonderful.

J. Dwight Pentecost (How's that for a cool name?) has a great book on the Person and work of the Holy Spirit. It's called *The Divine Comforter.*

The easy-to-understand book of theology is called *The Moody Handbook of Theology* by Paul Enns.

Moving On

In addition to showing you that the Holy Spirit is a divine Person who has been active through the history of the world, we hope we have helped you understand that the Holy Spirit isn't something impersonal for you to use. The Holy Spirit is God in Person who wants to use you. In the next chapter you're going to see how this works as we look at how the Holy Spirit works.

CHAPTER 2

WHAT IN THE WORLD IS THE HOLY SPIRIT DOING?

I should as soon attempt to raise flowers if there were no atmosphere, or produce fruits if there were neither light nor heat, as to regenerate men if I did not believe there was a Holy Spirit.

—Henry Ward Beecher

In chapter 1 we gave you some theology (discussing who the Holy Spirit is). We also sprinkled in some history (reviewing what He did in the Old Testament and in the life of Christ). So much for the academic and historical overview. Now it's time to get relevant to what is going on in your life (or at least going on in the world around you).

Up to the time when Jesus returned to heaven after His resurrection, the Holy Spirit kept a low profile. Not anymore. For the last two centuries, the Holy Spirit has been the part of the Trinity that has been most active on earth. And it gets even more relevant than that. More than just influencing changes in the world, the Holy Spirit may be at work right now changing you!

Aren't you curious to know what He's up to?

Bruce & Stan

Chapter 2

What in the World
Is the Holy Spirit Doing?

What's Ahead

- The Holy Spirit Came to Earth, and the Crowd Went Wild
- The Big Initiator
- It's an Inside Job
- All in the Family
- The Change Maker
- Signed, Sealed, and Delivered

It just so happens that we are writing this chapter while the NBA play-offs are going on. Each of us has a television in our office, but ordinarily we don't watch the games on TV while we are writing. (Stan has sufficient self-discipline to resist watching; Bruce can't watch because his wife removed the rearview mirror that he had attached to his monitor to see the television behind his back.) However, we figured we could justify watching the NBA finals if we could find an analogy between the NBA championship games and the Holy Spirit. So we did, and here it is (and it isn't even a stretch):

> The Holy Spirit is a lot like the reserve player on a team. At first, the starters get all of the attention. But when one of the stars gets taken out of the game, the reserve player comes off the bench and starts making great plays on the court. By making some unbelievable shots, that little-known reserve player becomes a hero by assuring the victory.

As we discussed in chapter 1, the Holy Spirit was the relatively unsung hero of the Trinity during all of history, until about 2000 years ago. Oh, sure, He got in a little playing time. But let's admit it: All of the publicity during Old Testament times went to God the Father. Then, when Jesus Christ came to earth, He started to get all the attention. He deserved it; after all, Jesus is the Savior of the human race, and He died on the cross to pay the penalty for our sins. His superstardom even increased when He came back to life on the third day after His crucifixion.

But in about A.D. 33, Jesus was "taken out of the game" when He returned to heaven. (Theologians refer to this event as the Ascension. It's a non-sports term, but what do you expect from a bunch of stuffy eggheads?) As the Player/Coach, God sent the Holy Spirit to earth to get into the game.

Jesus actually told His disciples that this "substitution" (Are we pushing the analogy too far?) was going to happen. They didn't really understand it at the time, but here is what He said as He explained that He was going to die, come back to life, and then return to heaven:

And I will ask the Father, and he will give you another Counselor, who will never leave you. He is the Holy Spirit, who leads into all truth. The world at large cannot receive him, because it isn't looking for him and doesn't recognize him. But you do, because he lives with you now and later will be in you (John 14:16,17).

And it happened, just as Jesus said it would.

The Holy Spirit Came to Earth, and the Crowd Went Wild

There was a delay of seven weeks between the time that Christ returned to heaven and when the Holy Spirit came to earth. But the arrival of the Holy Spirit was so spectacular that there was no chance that anybody would miss it or mistake it for something else. The supernatural phenomenon that occurred is often referred to as Pentecost (which sounds like "penny cost"), because it occurred on the Jewish holiday known as the Feast of Pentecost.

Factoid: The Jews celebrated the Feast of Pentecost to commemorate God giving the law to Moses. Bible scholars have said that it is no mere coincidence that the Holy Spirit arrived on the day of Pentecost. The sacrifice of Christ on the cross replaced the law, so now we can celebrate God giving the Holy Spirit to us.

Here is the report of what happened that morning at Pentecost:

On the day of Pentecost, seven weeks after Jesus' resurrection, the believers were meeting together in one place. Suddenly, there was a sound from heaven like the roaring of a mighty windstorm in the skies above them, and it filled the house where they were meeting. Then, what looked like flames or tongues of fire appeared and settled on each of them. And everyone present was filled with the Holy Spirit and began speaking in other languages, as the Holy Spirit gave them this ability (Acts 2:1-4).

Talk about making a grand entrance! The roar of wind, the appearance of fire, and speaking in different languages is enough to draw a large crowd of spectators, and that is exactly what happened. And it was immediately evident to the crowd that those believers weren't just spouting out a bunch of gibberish. The residents of Jerusalem who were immigrants from foreign countries recognized their native languages. This was all part of the divine plan to prove the supernatural existence of God and to spread the message that Jesus Christ is the way of salvation. How convenient that the Holy Spirit also provided the message in multiple languages so that nothing would be lost in the translation.

> *Godly Jews from many nations were living in Jerusalem at that time. When they heard this sound, they came running to see what it was all about, and they were bewildered*

> *to hear their own languages being spoken*
> *by the believers. They were beside them-*
> *selves with wonder. "How can this be?"*
> *they exclaimed. "These people are all from*
> *Galilee, and yet we hear them speaking the*
> *languages of the lands where we were*
> *born!…And we all hear these people*
> *speaking in our own languages about the*
> *wonderful things God has done!"* (Acts
> 2:5-8,11).

Of course, there are always a few skeptics
in every crowd, and this situation was no
different:

> *But others in the crowd were mocking.*
> *"They're drunk, that's all!" they said*
> (Acts 2:13).

Although the disciple Peter had wimped
out and denied Jesus on the evening before
the crucifixion, the Holy Spirit made him
bold on this occasion. He got the crowd's
attention and explained what was going on:

> *Then Peter stepped forward with the*
> *eleven other apostles and shouted to the*
> *crowd, "Listen carefully, all of you, fellow*
> *Jews and residents of Jerusalem! Make no*
> *mistake about this. Some of you are saying*

these people are drunk. It isn't true! It's much too early for that. People don't get drunk by nine o'clock in the morning" (Acts 2:14,15).

Peter went on to explain that this miracle was another step in God's progressive plan to reveal that salvation is available to the people of the world through Jesus Christ:

People of Israel, listen! God publicly endorsed Jesus of Nazareth by doing wonderful miracles, wonders, and signs through him, as you well know. But you followed God's prearranged plan. With the help of lawless Gentiles, you nailed him to the cross and murdered him. However, God released him from the horrors of death and raised him back to life again, for death could not keep him in its grip....Now he sits on the throne of highest honor in heaven, at God's right hand. And the Father, as he had promised, gave him the Holy Spirit to pour out upon us, just as you see and hear today (Acts 2:22-24,33).

The sight of flames, the sounds of the foreign languages, and the sense of Peter's sermon were enough to impress the crowd that a God thing was happening. They wanted to know how they should respond.

> Peter replied, "Each of you must turn from your sins and turn to God, and be baptized in the name of Jesus Christ for the forgiveness of your sins. Then you will receive the gift of the Holy Spirit. This promise is to you and to your children, and even to the Gentiles—all who have been called by the Lord our God" (Acts 2:38,39).

 The events of Pentecost mark the beginning of the Holy Spirit's involvement in the lives of those who believe and follow Christ. And the Holy Spirit has been at it ever since. Sometimes you'll know—without a doubt—that He is working because the results are supernatural. Other times He is a bit more inconspicuous (we doubt that you've seen a flame of fire over your head). But all that He does, conspicuous or not, is spectacular. So that you don't miss any aspect of His amazing activities, it will take the rest of

Factoid: *Don't think that Pentecost was some little Holy Roller church gathering with a few bystanders who got caught up in the excitement and the emotion. The Bible says that 3000 people believed what Peter said* (Acts 2:41).

this book for us to give you a brief overview. For the remainder of this chapter, we'll be explaining what the Holy Spirit accomplishes in your life the moment you accept Christ as your Savior.

The Big Initiator

Anyone who has ever believed in Jesus as Savior has the Holy Spirit to thank. You can't take credit for it yourself, because the Holy Spirit was the One who initiated the entire process.

The moment a person believes in Christ as Savior, he or she has a spiritual life. In this section we'll be talking about the process by which the Holy Spirit accomplished that transformation. From a human perspective, it is all about *conversion.* From God's perspective, it is all about *regeneration.* Regardless of the perspective, the Holy Spirit is the One who makes it happen.

Conversion

Conversion happens when a person turns to God. There are two aspects to conversion:

1. Conversion involves *repentance* (regretting your past sins and turning away from them toward God); and

2. Conversion involves *faith* (accepting the promises of Christ as true and believing in His saving power).

Repentance and faith are brought about by the Holy Spirit. All people are buried so deeply in their sin nature that they can't turn to God in their own power. Jesus explained to the disciples that the Holy Spirit would be the One to turn people's hearts and minds toward Christ:

> *And when he comes, he will convince the world of its sin, and of God's righteousness, and of the coming judgment. The world's sin is unbelief in me* (John 16:8,9).

The failure to believe in God is the greatest of all sins. That unbelief can be removed only by the Holy Spirit's power. Without this convicting work of the Holy Spirit, there would be no conversion.

Regeneration

The term *regeneration* sounds like something that would happen at an electrical power plant when garbage and trash are recycled into usable materials. In a spiritual sense, that is exactly what happens. As theologian Millard J. Erickson said:

> Regeneration is the miraculous trans-
> formation of the individual and im-
> plantation of spiritual energy.

In other words, without Christ our lives
are about as useless and powerless as trash.
But through the energizing, recycling work
of the Holy Spirit, you can be remade into
something useful to God. (It's the new and
improved you!)

Jesus made it very clear that regeneration
is essential if we are going to be considered acceptable to God. That isn't something that *we* can accomplish. It takes the
Holy Spirit to pull it off. Here is how
Jesus laid it out for a seeker by the name
of Nicodemus:

> *Jesus replied, "I assure you, unless you are
> born again, you can never see the
> Kingdom of God."*
>
> *"What do you mean?" exclaimed
> Nicodemus. "How can an old man go back
> into his mother's womb and be born
> again?"*
>
> *Jesus replied, "The truth is, no one can
> enter the Kingdom of God without being
> born of water and the Spirit. Humans can*

reproduce only human life, but the Holy Spirit gives new life from heaven" (John 3:3-6).

Jesus emphasized that regeneration was a supernatural process. In that process, the Holy Spirit leads and enables the person to accept Jesus as Savior and gives the person a new spiritual nature within.

 Are you wondering how this whole "regeneration" thing works? Are you curious about how a person actually gets reborn spiritually? So are we. Don't fret because you can't figure it out. It is just enough to know that the Holy Spirit can take care of it for you. As Jesus told someone who wanted to know:

Just as you can hear the wind but can't tell where it comes from or where it is going, so you can't explain how people are born of the Spirit (John 3:8).

It's an Inside Job

The work of the Holy Spirit doesn't end when a person becomes a believer. That just marks the beginning of what the Holy Spirit does.

As you might expect, the Holy Spirit can be found whenever believers gather together. The church, meaning a collective group of believers (not the building), is the dwelling place of the Holy Spirit:

> *Don't you realize that all of you together are the temple of God and that the Spirit of God lives in you?* (1 Corinthians 3:16).

But the Holy Spirit gets much more personal with each individual believer than merely being a chaperon at church gatherings. The Holy Spirit actually lives inside each believer. Of course, the Holy Spirit won't show up on a CAT scan or in an X-ray, and you can't use Him as an excuse for that bloated feeling you've had recently. But if you are a follower of Christ, the Holy Spirit is present in your life.

This role of the Holy Spirit is referred to as His *indwelling*. (Even *we* can understand how the theologians came up with that term.) Think of it as if your body is a temple for the Holy Spirit. That is not our analogy; it is in the Bible:

> *Or don't you know that your body is the temple of the Holy Spirit, who lives in you*

and was given to you by God? (1 Corinthians 6:19).

Think about these two significant consequences of the Holy Spirit indwelling your life:

1. You should be mindful that the Spirit of God lives within you. If you are doing things or going places that you shouldn't, you are dragging God along into that mess.

2. If you relinquish control of your life to God, He can help you avoid worldly temptations because His Spirit lives within you.

But you are not controlled by your sinful nature. You are controlled by the Spirit if you have the Spirit of God living in you. (And remember that those who do not have the Spirit of Christ living in them are not Christians at all.) Since Christ lives within you, even though your body will die because of sin, your spirit is alive because you have been made right with God. The Spirit of God, who raised Jesus from the dead, lives in you. And just as he raised Christ from the dead, he will give life to your mortal body by this same Spirit living within you (Romans 8:9-11).

ONCE AND FOREVER

What about the person who believes in Jesus (and therefore has the Holy Spirit) but subsequently sins? Does the Holy Spirit leave you the moment you commit a sinful act? That's a good question, but it is one that is easily answered: *No!* But you don't have to take our word for it.

- If you lost the Holy Spirit when you sinned, then you wouldn't be saved anymore because "those who do not have the Spirit of Christ living in them are not Christians at all." (See Romans 8:9 again.) But you can't lose your salvation. Jesus promised that once you belong to Him, He'll never let you go (John 6:37). And as Paul explained, there is *nothing* (and that would include our own sin) that can separate us from the love of God (Romans 8:31-39).

- When Jesus was telling His disciples about the Holy Spirit, He said, "And I will ask the Father, and he will give you another Counselor, who will never leave you" (John 14:16). *Never* means "never"—not even when we sin.

All in the Family

After His resurrection and just before He returned to heaven, Jesus gave a few last-minute reminders to His disciples. Although He had told them about the Holy Spirit at dinner on the night before He was crucified, Jesus probably knew that these guys were a little dense and could use a reminder.

> *In one of these meetings as he was eating a meal with them, he told them, "Do not leave Jerusalem until the Father sends you what he promised. Remember, I have told you about this before. John baptized with water, but in just a few days you will be baptized with the Holy Spirit"* (Acts 1:4,5).

Did you notice the word *baptized?* That is a very descriptive way to explain what happened at Pentecost. Just as people are drenched with water at a baptism (whether it is of the sprinkling variety or the dunking kind), the people at Pentecost were doused with the Holy Spirit. They were soaked with the Holy Spirit.

Another function of the Holy Spirit is referred to as *the baptism of the Holy Spirit.* It describes the Holy Spirit's role of bringing all believers together as part of the body of Christ.

- By His indwelling, the Holy Spirit becomes a part of the life of every believer.

- By His baptism, all believers become a part of the body of Christ.

This terminology is not as figurative as you might expect. Sure, we aren't a part of the body of Christ as in an ear, an elbow, or the pancreas. But we are a part of His body in the sense that we are risen with Him to newness of life:

> *Or have you forgotten that when we became Christians and were baptized to become one with Christ Jesus, we died with him? For we died and were buried with Christ by baptism. And just as Christ was raised from the dead by the glorious power of the Father, now we also may live new lives* (Romans 6:3,4).

Being part of the body of Christ has several distinct consequences:

- We are joined with all other believers as part of Christ's body. Therefore, we should seek to live in unity and harmony with other Christians. (Imagine how painful it would be if your liver and your kidneys were antagonistic toward each other.)

> *Always keep yourselves united in the Holy Spirit, and bind yourselves together with*

peace. We are all one body, we have the same Spirit, and we have all been called to the same glorious future. There is only one Lord, one faith, one baptism, and there is only one God and Father, who is over us all and in us all and living through us all (Ephesians 4:3-6).

• Because we all work together within the body of Christ, each of us needs to do our respective jobs. The Holy Spirit has given to each of us a "spiritual gift" (more about this in chapter 4) that is to be used within the body of Christ. If we don't use it, the entire body suffers. (Imagine what your life would be like if your various body parts simply decided to slack off and shut down whenever they got a little lazy. You better hope your heart doesn't get that attitude.) The Holy Spirit is the One who oversees the administration of each Christian working within the body of Christ.

Under his direction, the whole body is fitted together perfectly. As each part does its own special work, it helps the other parts grow, so that the whole body is healthy and growing and full of love (Ephesians 4:16).

- As part of the body of Christ, we are connected to His death, burial, and resurrection. For that reason, we should be anxious to separate ourselves from sinful activities and attitudes.

  Well then, should we keep on sinning so that God can show us more and more kindness and forgiveness? Of course not! Since we have died to sin, how can we continue to live in it? Or have you forgotten that when we became Christians and were baptized to become one with Christ Jesus, we died with him?…Since we have been united with him in his death, we will also be raised as he was. Our old sinful selves were crucified with Christ so that sin might lose its power in our lives.…So you should consider yourselves dead to sin and able to live for the glory of God through Christ Jesus (Romans 6:1-3,5,6,11).

The Change Maker

Both of us are dads; we each have a son and a daughter. Our kids are old enough to have given us the privilege—and the occasional agony—of seeing them mature into something resembling adult people. It didn't happen all at once. It was a process.

Most of the time they made good progress. On rare occasions, they messed up (which they now blame on poor fathering skills).

Your spiritual relationship with God also requires a growing maturity. It is a process that happens over time. Hopefully, you will make good progress. Every once in a while you will mess up (but the fault will be all yours, so don't try to blame it on poor heavenly fathering skills).

The Holy Spirit is available to help you in the process of becoming spiritually mature:

- He can give you spiritual insight and guide you in truth (John 16:12-15). We go into detail on this subject in chapter 3.

- He can assist you in praying according to the will of God (Romans 8:26; Ephesians 6:18).

- He empowers you with one or more spiritual gifts (1 Corinthians 12:7)— more about this in chapter 4.

- He equips you for spiritual battle against temptation and the forces of Satan (Romans 8:13; Galatians 5:16,17).

If the process of spiritual progress is slow, some people complain that they need to get more of the Holy Spirit in their life. They have got it all wrong. Spiritual maturity is never a question of getting more of the Holy Spirit. If you are a believer, you already have all of Him. The question is just the opposite: "How much of you does the Holy Spirit have?"

The apostle Paul knew that we will make progress with our spiritual maturity only when we make our entire lives available to the Holy Spirit. The more control we allow Him in our lives, the more Christlike our lives will become. This concept is referred to as "being filled with the Holy Spirit":

> *So be careful how you live, not as fools but as those who are wise. Make the most of every opportunity for doing good in these evil days. Don't act thoughtlessly, but try to understand what the Lord wants you to do....Instead, let the Holy Spirit fill and control you* (Ephesians 5:15-18).

In the next chapter we'll be talking about the characteristics of a Spirit-filled life. As a teaser, we'll tell you that the Holy Spirit can give you:

- A Christlike character

- A desire to make sure that other people know the good news about Jesus

- An enthusiasm for praising, thanking, and worshiping God

 Sometimes people get confused by the distinctions between the baptism of the Holy Spirit and the filling of the Holy Spirit. In his book *Basic Theology*, Charles Ryrie clarifies the differences. Here are a few of the distinctions that he identifies:

Spirit Baptism	Spirit Filling
Occurs only once in each believer's life	Is a repeated experience
True of all believers	Not necessarily experienced by all
Cannot be undone	Can be lost
Results in a *position*	Results in *power*
Occurs when we believe in Christ	Occurs throughout the Christian life
No prerequisite (except faith in Christ)	Depends on yieldedness

Signed, Sealed, and Delivered

The Holy Spirit *seals* believers. Those who truly put their faith in Christ are given a "seal of approval" by the Holy Spirit. You aren't branded like cattle, but you are considered by God as His, and He is never going to discard you out of His family (not even if you blow it from time to time, which all of us do). This aspect of belonging to God forever is referred to as the "sealing work" of the Holy Spirit.

If God won't kick us out of His family, then we can be as bad as we want to be without risking our eternal destiny, right? That is technically correct (although how can you truly love Christ if you live in continual defiance with no remorse). Because God loves us unconditionally, our response ought to be one of appreciation shown by living according to godly principles. The apostle Paul made this very point as he explained the sealing work of the Holy Spirit:

> *And do not bring sorrow to God's Holy Spirit by the way you live. Remember, he is the one who has identified you as his own, guaranteeing that you will be saved on the day of redemption* (Ephesians 4:30).

"What's That Again?"

1. Jesus didn't abandon His followers when He returned to heaven. He sent the Holy Spirit as a spiritual guide and companion. The first occurrence of the Holy Spirit in this role was at an event known as Pentecost, where the power of the Holy Spirit was revealed by supernatural events.

2. People turn to God only because the Holy Spirit convicts them of sin; there would be no conversion without the work of the Holy Spirit. And the Holy Spirit works the regeneration in our lives by which we are spiritually reborn.

3. The Holy Spirit is in the life ("indwells") of every believer. We don't lose the presence of the Holy Spirit when we sin.

4. As believers, we are "baptized" into the body of Christ by the Holy Spirit. This means that we are united with God and united with all other believers.

5. If we want to mature spiritually, we need to be "filled" by the Holy Spirit. This means allowing Him to have control of our life.

6. The Holy Spirit "seals" our salvation. It is a lifetime guarantee.

Dig Deeper

 Sometimes the best place to find an overview of information about the Holy Spirit is in a systematic theology reference book that explains all about God and His plan for the universe (in general) and you (in particular). Here are three that you could check out:

1. The *Lewis Sperry Chafer Systematic Theology* set (two volumes) devotes about 40 pages specifically to the Holy Spirit.

2. Don't be intimidated by the thickness of *Christian Theology* by Millard J. Erickson. The print is small, but you'll enjoy the content.

3. *Basic Theology* by Charles C. Ryrie has ten chapters on the Holy Spirit. (Don't worry; they're short chapters.)

Moving On

Don't you wish that there was someone who could help you understand what you read in the Bible? Would you appreciate a person who would not only explain what you read, but who would also help you apply it to your personal circumstances? If a person knew that much about the Bible, maybe you could ask that same individual for a little help with the other areas of your life. Well, that person exists, and He is the Holy Spirit.

In addition to all the work that we discussed in this chapter, the Holy Spirit has the role of guiding you in life. It is a very personal relationship that the Holy Spirit has with you, but He doesn't want to be the center of all your attention. In fact, His goal is to direct your focus to Jesus. Chapter 3 is all about the ways in which the Holy Spirit guides you (if you let Him).

CHAPTER 3

THE COACH WHO KEEPS YOU GROWING

No eye has seen, no ear has heard, and no mind has imagined what God has prepared for those who love him.

—1 Corinthians 2:9

Everybody needs a coach—that is, if you want to get anywhere in life. Coaches have different names. Sometimes they are called teachers, mentors, advisers, or even counselors. We like *coach* because it gives you the image of someone who stops bad habits and then trains you to do something better than you did before.

How about you? Do you have a coach, a mentor, or a teacher who is helping to make you a better person? If you don't, we have the perfect candidate, and we have a feeling you already know who He is.

Bruce & Stan

Chapter 3

The Coach Who Keeps You Growing

What's Ahead

➤ Your Spiritual Helper
➤ Your Spiritual Guide
➤ Your Spiritual Teacher
➤ The Fruit of the Spirit
➤ The Holy Spirit and Holiness

*A*ll of the great athletes have great coaches. Phil Jackson has coached both Michael Jordan and Shaquille O'Neal. Even Tiger Woods has a coach. Bruce & Stan have…No, wait—that can't be! We aren't great athletes. Hey, we aren't even athletes, but we do have at least two coaches, who will remain nameless at the risk of embarrassing them.

The likelihood of any of us convincing a great coach to work with us is pretty small. That's because great coaches don't take on the job of training someone unless they see enormous potential, which narrows the field down to very few people (mainly people who have enormous *earning* potential). But don't worry that a great coach will never show you how to swing a golf club. Don't lose sleep over the fact that Bobby Knight will never show you how to fling a folding chair across a basketball court. You've got someone much better who wants to coach you.

He's the Holy Spirit—the world's greatest Coach—who is ready, willing, and able to take you on because He sees tremendous potential in you. He wants to take you from your current state of spiritual mediocrity to something far beyond anything you could imagine. He's got all the time in the world for you. All you have to do is make yourself available as you learn how and where the Holy Spirit works. Let's take a look at the different ways the Holy Spirit coaches us.

COACH PARACLETE

When Jesus walked the earth, He was the world's greatest Coach. He worked with a team of guys known as the Disciples (they played in the Middle Eastern division). Over a period of three years, Jesus transformed them from insecure losers to bold proclaimers. Toward the end of His time on earth, Jesus told the disciples that He was going to be stepping down as their Coach. But He wasn't going to leave them coachless. "I will ask the Father, and he will give you another Counselor, who will never leave you. He is the Holy Spirit" (John 14:16,17).

The name *counselor* is another word for *coach*. But an even better name is *paraclete*, which is the Greek word Jesus used. A paraclete is someone who comes alongside you as a companion to counsel, comfort, instruct, and advise you—everything a great coach should be. So when you think of the Holy Spirit, think of *Paraclete*, someone who has stepped in for Jesus as your nearest and closest Coach.

Your Spiritual Helper

Like the great Coach that He is, the Holy Spirit helps you in every spiritual way possible. By definition, a helper is someone who makes it possible to do something that you can't do alone. (As an example, Bruce helps Stan write, and Stan helps Bruce write. We do this because neither of us can write on our own.) A helper provides assistance, advice, direction, and comfort. That's what the Holy Spirit does, especially in four critical areas.

1. The Holy Spirit helps you pray.

Prayer is such an important activity for the Christian because it's the way you talk with God and tell Him your greatest needs and your deepest desires. It's how you ask God for direction. And yet how many times have you tried to pray, and you just didn't know what to say, or you prayed and you didn't feel like you were getting through to God? What do you do? That's where the Holy Spirit comes in. As your Helper, the Holy Spirit does something utterly amazing for you:

And the Holy Spirit helps us in our distress. For we don't even know what we should pray for, nor how we should pray. But the Holy Spirit prays for us with groanings that cannot be expressed in words. And the Father who knows all hearts knows what the Spirit is saying, for the Spirit pleads for us believers in harmony with God's own will (Romans 8:26,27).

Do you see the incredible benefit here? When you get spiritually tongue-tied, the Holy Spirit steps in and prays for you in a spiritual language no words can duplicate.

This is an amazing mystery. Even though you don't know what to pray for, as you pray the Holy Spirit tells God what is in your heart, and God knows exactly what He is saying because the Holy Spirit is in complete harmony with God.

Not only does the Holy Spirit pray *for* you, but He also tells you what to pray for:

> *And continue to pray as you are directed by the Holy Spirit* (Jude 20).

2. The Holy Spirit helps you love.

The Holy Spirit doesn't work with loners. When God saved you, you were automatically baptized by the Holy Spirit into the body of Christ so that you could serve and love other Christians (1 Corinthians 12:13). In fact, our service and love for other Christians proves to the world that we are followers of Christ (John 13:35).

If that seems tough to do sometimes, you can thank God that He has given you the Holy Spirit to help you love (1 John 4:11-14).

3. The Holy Spirit helps you worship.

God deserves all the praise and worship we can give Him, but it isn't something that comes naturally. We need help, and God knows it. That's why He has given us the Holy Spirit to lead us into worship (Philippians 3:3). Jesus told the Samaritan woman, "For God is Spirit, so those who worship him must worship in spirit and in truth" (John 4:24). Whether you are in church worshiping with other believers, or you are alone in your quiet time, the Holy Spirit will help you worship God in a way that pleases Him.

4. The Holy Spirit helps you in your stress.

Let's face it. Life is full of a lot of worry and stress. Even though the Bible tells us not to worry, it's tough to give our concerns over to God. We somehow think that if we hang onto our troubles, they'll get better (and they never do). That's where the Holy Spirit comes in. As your ultimate Coach, the Holy Spirit promises to comfort you as you walk with the Lord (Acts 9:31). He promises to help you when you are mentally, physically, or emotionally stressed (Romans 8:26).

Another important area where the Holy Spirit provides comfort is in your salvation. At one time or another, you are going to wonder if you are truly saved. It is completely normal to have doubts about your salvation, but that's not something you have to live with all the time. Pray and ask

God to comfort you through the Holy Spirit. Ask God to assure you that you are saved, and He will do it.

> *For his Holy Spirit speaks to us deep in our hearts and tells us that we are God's children* (Romans 8:16).

Your Spiritual Guide

Do you want to know God's will for your life? Hey, we all do! Only it doesn't come all at once. God's will is progressive, kind of like a good mystery novel, except you can't skip ahead to see what's going to happen next. You have to take it one day at a time. As much as you would like to believe that God's will is about knowing the big stuff in life such as your career, your relationships, and your family, it's really more about walking daily with the Lord, as the Holy Spirit guides you step-by-step (somehow the big stuff takes care of itself).

Imagine that you have hired a guide to take you on a treacherous path to the top of a mountain. No guide worth his salt would simply meet you at the end of the trail and wait for you to get there. A helpful guide walks beside you or slightly ahead of you, showing you where to put your steps and pointing out the dangers to avoid. That's what the Holy Spirit does.

If we are living now by the Holy Spirit, let us follow the Holy Spirit's leading in every part of our lives (Galatians 5:25).

The Holy Spirit will guide you in a variety of ways. He will use your circumstances, even the little things that seem insignificant. "The steps of the godly are directed by the LORD," wrote King David. "He delights in every detail of their lives" (Psalm 37:23). Another way is through the wise counsel of spiritually mature Christians. The wisest man who ever lived wrote: "Plans go wrong for lack of advice; many counselors bring success" (Proverbs 15:22). God even uses your thoughts and your desires to guide you. But be careful. This is a very subjective area. Your thoughts and desires are a valid guide only if they are centered on God in the first place (Psalm 37:4).

As important as these guides are—your circumstances, other Christians, and your own inclinations—they are no substitute for the most reliable and most common way the Holy Spirit guides and teaches you: through the Word of God.

Your Spiritual Teacher

It's nearly impossible to teach someone unless he is willing to learn, and you can't learn very well unless you are willing to study and practice—whether it's basketball, golf, or physics. For the Christian, the very best way to learn what the Holy Spirit wants to teach you is to study God's Word and practice what it says.

All Scripture is inspired by God and is useful to teach us what is true and to make us realize what is wrong in our lives. It straightens us out and teaches us to do what is right. It is God's way of preparing us in every way, fully equipped for every good thing God wants us to do (2 Timothy 3:16,17).

If you want the Holy Spirit to guide you and teach you the incredible truths about God and what He wants you to do, you have to read and study the Bible. Just like prayer is the way you talk to God (with the help of the Holy Spirit), the Bible is the way God talks to you (with the help of the Holy Spirit).

> *But we know these things because God has revealed them to us by his Spirit, and his*

Spirit searches out everything and shows us even God's deep secrets. No one can know what anyone else is really thinking except that person alone, and no one can know God's thoughts except God's own Spirit. And God has actually given us his Spirit (not the world's spirit) so we can know the wonderful things God has freely given us (1 Corinthians 2:10-12).

In a very real sense, the Holy Spirit is a teacher of truth. He doesn't just help us to see the truth by opening our minds to receive it. The Holy Spirit personally comes to us and teaches us the Word of God so that we can learn and teach other people.

Breathing In, Breathing Out

In chapter 2 we talked about how God used the Holy Spirit to breathe in *His Word* into 40 different authors who wrote down His personal message for us. In the same way, God uses the Holy Spirit to breathe out *His Word* directly into our minds and hearts so we can understand what He wants us to do.

When we tell you this, we do not use words of human wisdom. We speak words given to us by the Spirit, using the Spirit's words to explain spiritual truths (1 Corinthians 2:13).

Have you ever wrestled with a passage of Scripture, and then suddenly the meaning dawns on you? That's the Holy Spirit opening your understanding. Have you ever been in a conversation with someone and you say something very profound about the Lord, and you wonder, "Where did that come from?" That's the Holy Spirit giving you the words to say.

WHY DOESN'T EVERYONE GET IT?

There's a reason why Christians sometimes seem like fools to non-Christians. They just don't get it. By "they" we mean anyone who does not have a personal relationship with God through Jesus Christ. You could be the smartest person in the world, and you still wouldn't be able to grasp the "deep secrets" of God. Here's why:

> *But people who aren't Christians can't under-stand these truths from God's Spirit. It all sounds foolish to them because only those who have the Spirit can understand what the Spirit means. We who have the Spirit understand these things, but others can't understand us at all.... But we can understand these things, for we have the mind of Christ* (1 Corinthians 2:14-16).

So don't be distressed when someone like Ted Turner calls Christians a bunch of fools and losers, or some film producer portrays Christians as a bunch of raving lunatics. That's the only perspective they have.

The Fruit of the Spirit

Until now in this pocket guide, we have shown you who the Holy Spirit is and how He works in the world and in your life. Now it's time for a major shift. Starting here and continuing to the end of the book, we are going to suggest ways for you to show the spiritual character qualities and exercise the spiritual gifts that the Holy Spirit has given you. We're going to cover spiritual gifts in chapter 4. Right now let's concentrate on nine spiritual character qualities, known as the fruit of the Spirit.

> *The fruit of the Spirit are character qualities that God possesses and that the Holy Spirit imparts to us as we live in trusting obedience to Jesus.*
> —Max Anders

In his book *Secrets of the Vine,* Bruce Wilkinson writes this about the fruit of the Spirit:

> In practical terms, fruit represents good works—a thought, attitude, or action of ours that God values because it glorifies Him. The fruit from your life is how God receives His due honor on earth. That's why Jesus declares, "By this My Father is glorified, that you bear much fruit" (John 15:8).

Fruit and good works are mentioned several times in the Bible, but the most well-known verses are found in Galatians:

But when the Holy Spirit controls our lives, he will produce this kind of fruit in us: love, joy, peace, patience, kindness, goodness, faithfulness, gentleness, and self-control (Galatians 5:22,23).

We're going to follow Billy Graham's method of dividing these nine character qualities into three "clusters" of three fruit. Each cluster represents a different relationship.

Fruit Cluster #1: Love, Joy, Peace: Your "Godward" Relationship

The greatest of all Christian virtues is *love* (1 Corinthians 13:13), so it's appropriate that this quality leads the list. First we are to love God. Jesus said, "You must love the Lord your God with all your heart, all your soul, and all your mind. This is the first and greatest commandment" (Matthew 22:37,38). Then we are to love our neighbor (Matthew 22:39) and other Christians (John 13:35). We are to model our love after God, who Himself is love (1 John 4:8). We should love with the same sacrificial love that motivated God to send Jesus into the world (John 3:16).

The world strives for happiness, but Christians should seek *joy.* The difference is that happiness depends on outward circumstances (winning the lottery, having a baby, watching the Lakers win the NBA Championship), whereas joy is based on obeying Jesus and knowing that He loves us. "I have told you this so that you will be filled with joy," Jesus said. "Yes, your joy will overflow!" (John 15:11). Joy isn't affected by the negative stuff that happens in your life. In fact, when you suffer—especially when you suffer for being a Christian— you can rejoice, "for then the glorious Spirit of God will come upon you" (1 Peter 4:14).

Everyone wants *peace,* but peace between people and nations is only temporary. In a world torn by strife, we need to show the peace of God, "which is far more wonderful than the human mind can understand" (Philippians 4:7). The peace that comes from the Holy Spirit will keep us united with our fellow Christians (Ephesians 4:3) and everyone else (Hebrews 12:14).

No Such Thing as *Fruits* of the Spirit

In chapter 4 you're going to see that all Christians do not have all the *gifts* of the Spirit. The gifts are divided among believers. By contrast, all of the *fruit* of the Spirit are for all believers. That's why you'll never see the Bible talk about *fruits*. Your goal should be to have all the character qualities, not just a few.

Fruit Cluster #2: Patience, Kindness, Goodness: Your "Outward" Relationship

You don't develop *patience* when everything goes your way and people are doing what you want them to do. It's when circumstances and people turn against you—that's when you need the kind of patience that only God can give you through the Holy Spirit.

> *We also pray that you will be strengthened with his glorious power so that you will have all the patience and endurance you need (Colossians 1:11).*

A few years ago someone wrote a little book called *Random Acts of Kindness.* There's nothing random about spiritual *kindness.* It's a deliberate act of treating others fairly even when they treat you rudely. To have this attitude means treating them the way God does. It means helping another Christian get "back onto the right path" (Galatians 6:1). It means that we "share each other's troubles and problems" (Galatians 6:2).

Sometimes you'll hear that someone did something out of the "goodness of his heart." That gets to the "heart" of *goodness*, which is more like generosity than kindness. When you help someone, not because he deserves it, but because you want to, this is goodness.

Fruit Cluster #3: Faithfulness, Gentleness, Self-Control: Your "Inward" Relationship

Faithfulness is different than faith. You exercise faith when you believe in God's plan to save you through Jesus (Ephesians 2:8), but the Holy Spirit produces the fruit of faithfulness in you when you let Him fill you. To be faithful means you are "entirely trustworthy and good" (Titus 2:10). If you are faithful, you are a person of your word as well as a person of God's Word.

There's nothing wimpy about someone who displays the character trait of *gentleness*. Jesus commended the gentle "for the whole earth will belong to them" (Matthew 5:5). Billy Graham compares a gentle person to a wild horse that has been tamed. The power is still there, but it's under control. Dr. James Boice writes that gentle people "are always angry at the right time (such as against sin) and never angry at the wrong time."

The final characteristic is *self-control*, which enables you to have mastery over your thoughts and actions. If you have spiritual self-control, you let the Holy Spirit control your life (Galatians 5:22). Without self-control, you end up following "the desires of your sinful nature," and that's not a pretty sight (Galatians 5:19-21). In fact, the desires of the sinful nature are the "default setting" in every Christian's life. To overcome what comes naturally, you need to make a choice every day and in every way to "live according to your new life in the Holy Spirit" (Galatians 5:16).

The Holy Spirit and Holiness

No one said living the Christian life was easy. You will always struggle in your war against your old sinful nature. But you don't have to struggle at the same level throughout your life. You can make progress toward a more mature and truly spiritual life as you grow in the Lord. And you don't have to do it alone. As your Coach, the Holy Spirit will make you into a better person as you allow Him to fill your life.

One of the primary activities of the Holy Spirit is to cleanse you from sin and to sanctify you. What that means is that He wants to make you more holy in your life. To be sanctified literally means to be set apart for God. As Paul explains:

> *There was a time when some of you were just like that, but now your sins have been washed away, and you have been set apart for God. You have been made right with God because of what the Lord Jesus Christ and the Spirit of our God have done for you* (1 Corinthians 6:11).

When you become a Christian, two things happen. First, Jesus and the Holy Spirit wash your sins away. Second, the Holy Spirit sanctifies you—He sets you apart— so He can begin the lifelong process of making you holy as He develops the fruit of the Spirit in your life.

This process of sanctification continues until the day you die or until Jesus returns, whichever comes first. Then and only then will you be completely holy. Until that day, the Holy Spirit will be working in you, and you will become "more and more like him and reflect his glory even more" (2 Corinthians 3:18).

"What's That Again?"

1. The Holy Spirit is the world's greatest Coach, who comes alongside to help, counsel, comfort, guide, and teach you.

2. The Holy Spirit guides you through circumstances, other mature Christians, and your inner convictions. But the most reliable way He guides you is through the Word of God.

3. The Holy Spirit opens your mind to receive the truth of Scripture, and He does even more. He personally comes and teaches you the Word of God so you can learn and teach other people.

4. There are nine spiritual qualities known collectively as the fruit of the Spirit. These are character qualities that the Holy Spirit gives you as you live in obedience to Jesus.

5. Throughout your life the Holy Spirit will be setting you apart so that you will become more and more like Jesus.

Dig Deeper

Max Anders has written a series of books on Bible basics. His book *The Holy Spirit* is almost as user-friendly as this one!

If you're one of the millions of people who read and appreciated *The Prayer of Jabez*, then you will also enjoy Bruce Wilkinson's follow-up book, *Secrets of the Vine*, which has some excellent ideas on bearing fruit.

We like the section on the Holy Spirit in Dr. James Boice's classic book *Foundation of the Christian Faith.*

Moving On

You're almost there—one chapter to go (aren't you sad?). We're going to cover some more "rubber meets the road" stuff that you will be able to apply to your life every single day. Most of all, you are going to get some clues as to the nature of your supernatural gift (or gifts). That's right. We said *super*natural. Whether you know it or not, you are a super human (at least in God's eyes). Find out how in chapter 4.

Chapter 4

The Energizer That Keeps You Going

The word "Comforter" as applied to the Holy Spirit needs to be translated by some vigorous term. Literally, it means "with strength." Jesus promised His followers that "The Strengthener" would be with them forever. This promise is no lullaby for the faint-hearted. It is a blood transfusion for courageous living.

—E. Paul Hovey

BRUCE & STAN SAY

Superman (Clark Kent's alter ego) had that superstrength and flying thing going for him; Spiderman could climb walls; and Professor X could read people's minds. What would it be like if *you* had some sort of superhuman power? You might just find out in this chapter.

The Holy Spirit gives "spiritual gifts" to believers. These gifts are nothing less than some sort of supernatural power that isn't available to mere humans (meaning those who don't believe in God and don't possess the Holy Spirit in their lives).

Could it be that you haven't yet unwrapped the most spectacular gift—and the only supernatural one—that you will ever receive? What are you waiting for? Go to the next page and see what the Holy Spirit has for you.

Bruce & Stan

Chapter 4

The Energizer That Keeps You Going

*T*ry to put yourself in the place of the disciples during the time that they were following Jesus around the countryside and watching Him perform miracles. If you were one of the disciples, then you were an eyewitness when:

- Jesus give sight to those who were blind and enabled the lame to walk;

- Jesus cured leprosy and other diseases; and

- He even brought the dead back to life.

And you would know from personal experience that His miracles weren't limited to the medical variety. If you were one of the disciples, then you were in the sinking ship when He controlled the elements of nature and calmed a storm simply by talking to it. (That ability would come in handy now if you lived in Florida during hurricane season.) And let's not forget about the time when you saw Jesus borrow a kid's bag lunch and miraculously multiply the food so it could feed thousands of people to the point where they were stuffed and lots of food was left over. (This is the miracle power that is desired by every parent who has teenagers.)

Have you put yourself into this mental picture? Now stay with it a little bit longer as you contemplate how you—as one of the disciples—reacted when you heard Jesus say these words to you:

The truth is, anyone who believes in me will do the same works I have done, and even greater works, because I am going to be with the Father. You can ask for anything in my name, and I will do it, because the work of the Son brings glory to the Father. Yes, ask anything in my name, and I will do it! (John 14:12-14).

Is it really possible that you could do "greater works" than Christ did? Maybe you heard Him wrong. After all, you know your own limitations. You don't have power over your own complexion, so how are you going to perform medical miracles? And you can't stop it from raining when you wash the car, and you can't balance your checkbook, so thinking that you can transcend the laws of nature is a bit unrealistic. But wait! Jesus said the same thing to you again when He gave you and the other disciples a little pep talk immediately before He ascended to heaven:

Do not leave Jerusalem until the Father sends you what he promised. Remember, I have told you about this before. John baptized with water, but in just a few days you will be baptized with the Holy Spirit....But when the Holy Spirit has come upon you, you will receive power and will tell people about me everywhere—in Jerusalem, throughout Judea, in Samaria, and to the ends of the earth (Acts 1:4,5,8).

Okay, now you can snap back to real life. But don't think that your real life is just a boring, dull, run-of-the-mill, namby-pamby kind of existence. If you have accepted

Christ as your Savior, then you have the supernatural power that Jesus was talking about.

 What did He mean that you would get "power" when you received the Holy Spirit?

The Ultimate Gift Giver

 The power that Jesus described to His disciples (and to you) is referred to as a "spiritual gift." The gift giver is the Holy Spirit. He not only delivers the gift, He is the One who picked it out. And He'll even show you how it works if you are interested enough to unwrap it and start to use it.

The Basics

You may be anxious to know what your spiritual gift is, but before we see what these spiritual gifts look like, let's get a general sense of how they operate and what they are used for:

- Spiritual gifts are distributed by the Holy Spirit as He chooses. He decides who gets what.

> *It is the one and only Holy Spirit who distributes these gifts. He alone decides which gift each person should have* (1 Corinthians 12:11).

- Every believer has at least one spiritual gift. Nobody is left out.

  > *God has given gifts to each of you from his great variety of spiritual gifts* (1 Peter 4:10).

- Every spiritual gift is intended for the benefit of the Christian community. Your spiritual gift isn't given to you for your own personal enjoyment. Instead, you are supposed to use it to help other people.

  > *A spiritual gift is given to each of us as a means of helping the entire church* (1 Corinthians 12:7).

What They Are and What They Aren't

A "spiritual gift" is a God-given, supernatural ability for service to others. It may take the form of a special power of performance, or maybe knowledge, or sensitivity.

Most of the teaching in the Bible about spiritual gifts comes from the apostle Paul (but the apostle Peter sneaks in a little mention about them, too). Here is how the gifts are listed in these different passages:

- Romans 12:6-8—*"God has given each of us the ability to do certain things well...."*
  - ✓ Prophecy ✓ Encouragement ✓ Mercy
  - ✓ Serving ✓ Giving
  - ✓ Teaching ✓ Leadership

- 1 Corinthians 12:4-11—*"Now there are different kinds of spiritual gifts..."*
  - ✓ Wisdom ✓ Healing ✓ Discernment
  - ✓ Knowledge ✓ Miracles ✓ Tongues
  - ✓ Faith ✓ Prophecy ✓ Interpretation

- Ephesians 4:11—*"He is the one who gave these gifts to the church..."*
  - ✓ Apostle ✓ Evangelist ✓ Teacher
  - ✓ Prophet ✓ Pastor

- 1 Peter 4:10,11—*"God has given gifts to each of you from his great variety of spiritual gifts. Manage them well so that God's generosity can flow through you...."*
  - ✓ Speaking ✓ Service

We will get to the definition of specific gifts in the next section. But before we go there, let's avoid some confusion by specifying what spiritual gifts are *not:*

- *A spiritual gift does not have anything to do with a place.* You don't have to use your gift only in a church building. Sure, the gift of serving may occur at the church property, but it is just as likely to happen in the homes of the people in the church and in your neighborhood.

- *A spiritual gift does not depend upon a position, role, or job.* You don't have to be a pastor in your church to have the gift of teaching. And the pastor may actually have a spiritual gift other than those of pastoring or teaching.

- *A spiritual gift is not a specialized technique.* Someone in your church may be an expert at playing the piano or designing the church's web site. These aren't spiritual gifts; they are just abilities that came through a lot of practice.

- *A spiritual gift is not a natural talent.* There may be some overlap, but a natural ability can be used for personal (or selfish) purposes, whereas a spiritual gift is used to serve the Christian community.

IS IT A TALENT OR A SPIRITUAL GIFT?

There are several distinctions between your natural talents and your spiritual gift. Here are three important ones:

1. Your natural abilities come from your parents as a matter of genetics; your spiritual gift comes from God and is unrelated to the gene pool you're swimming in.

2. Your natural abilities are with you from birth (although that talent for belching the "Star-Spangled Banner" may not manifest itself until you are in junior high school). Your spiritual gift is apparently given at the time you put God in control of your life.

3. You can use your natural abilities and talents as you see fit, to benefit yourself or other people (or for evil purposes, if your knack is safecracking). Your spiritual gift is for the benefit of other Christians.

Thanks, I Love It! What Is It?

In an attempt to help you define and compare the spiritual gifts listed in the four

New Testament passages, we have placed them into five categories based on what the gift *does*. We don't know if anyone else categorizes spiritual gifts in this fashion, but it helps us make sense of them.

Discerning Gifts—The Power to Know

- *Word of Knowledge:* Did you ever wonder how Jesus knew certain facts about a person that He never met before? (See the story about His conversation with the woman at the well in John 4:1-42.) The spiritual gift of a word of knowledge is the supernatural ability to know some fact that would be impossible to know except from divine revelation. This doesn't mean that you'll know all the information of the universe. God simply chooses to reveal a small bit of information that will be helpful in the situation, much like when the woman at the well believed what Jesus was saying because He knew certain things about her.

- *Word of Wisdom:* This gift is a Holy Spirit-inspired revelation of a solution to an immediate problem. It is receiving God's wisdom for dealing with a particular situation. While all Christians are to study the Bible so we have a sense of God's wisdom (which is different than the world's value system), this spiritual gift is a special infusion of wisdom at a particular point in time for a particular purpose.

• *Discernment:* Similar to the gift of wisdom, the spiritual gift of discernment is an extraordinary ability to discern truth. It protects the Christian community from accepting false teachings. (We aren't supposed to leave the subject of God's truth to the people who have this spiritual gift. All Christians are instructed to study the Bible and test all teaching against what the Scripture says.)

Dynamic Gifts—The Power to Do

• *Faith:* Every Christian should have faith in God and His sovereign plan and power. The spiritual gift of faith, however, is the ability to believe God for the supply of a very specific need.

• *Miracles:* Jesus performed miracles to demonstrate that He was God's Son. The apostles were given the authority to perform miracles to prove the authority of their message. While God works miracles on His own, the ability to perform miracles is a spiritual gift given to some people. Some scholars believe that this gift is primarily seen in parts of the world where the gospel message is being presented for the first time.

- *Healing:* Certainly God can heal someone of a medical problem whenever He chooses to do so, and the New Testament instructs us on how to pray for healing. But there is a spiritual gift of healing as well. As with the gift of miracles, it may be that the primary purpose of this gift is to demonstrate the authority of the message of Jesus Christ.

Declaring Gifts—The Power to Say

- *Prophecy:* In a general sense, prophecy refers to declaring God's message; in a technical sense, it refers to a specific message that God wants delivered to His people. There are many "prophets" mentioned in the Old Testament, and a few in the New Testament.

- *Tongues:* This is the supernatural gift of being able to speak in a language that is not known to the person who is speaking it. Pentecost is the best example of the demonstration of this gift. This gift needs to be accompanied by the gift of interpretation (unless there happens to be some foreign-language-speaking person present who can translate). Often this gift is referred to as "praying in the Spirit."

- *Interpretation:* This gift is the ability to interpret the message being spoken in tongues so that the group can understand what is being said. Because the Christians in the church at Corinth were getting out of line with the gift of tongues, Paul instructed that no one was to speak in tongues unless the message could be interpreted. (See 1 Corinthians 14:27-34 for the circumstances that he imposed for the use of the tongues gift.)

THE PROOF IS IN THE POWER

The supernatural power of the spiritual gifts can be proof that God is involved in your life. Here is how the apostle Paul explained it to the Christians at Corinth:

> *And my message and my preaching were very plain. I did not use wise and persuasive speeches, but the Holy Spirit was powerful among you. I did this so that you might trust the power of God rather than human wisdom* (1 Corinthians 2:4,5).

And he said it this way to the Christians in the city of Thessalonica:

> *For when we brought you the Good News, it was not only with words but also with power, for the Holy Spirit gave you full assurance that what we said was true* (1 Thessalonians 1:5).

Other people may see God at work in your life through the spiritual gift that God has given to you. But more than anyone else, *you* will be impressed with God's presence and power in your life as you realize that things are happening that you couldn't do on your own.

Discipling Gifts—The Power to Instruct

- *Apostleship: Apostle* means "one who is sent." In a technical sense, it refers to the disciples who followed Christ while He was on earth, and then established the churches after Pentecost. Paul and Barnabas established churches also, and the term extends to them as well. Some scholars believe that this spiritual gift is not applicable now; others believe it may be found in those who are establishing churches around the world, just as the early apostles did.

- *Pastoring:* This gift is a special ability to lead, care for, and protect the people in the local church. This is often referred to as "shepherding the flock" because the shepherd has the responsibility of leading, feeding, and protecting the sheep.

- *Teaching:* Many people are put in positions that require them to teach. If they have the spiritual gift of teaching, then they have a supernatural ability to explain the truth of God's Word in a way that is correct but also relevant and practical.

- *Exhortation:* This is the ability to encourage people in their spiritual lives. Sometimes encouragement takes the form of supporting someone; sometimes it means to admonish them. Either way, it involves spiritual sensitivity.

- *Evangelism:* Evangelism usually refers to proclaiming the gospel message to those who haven't heard it before. This spiritual gift is the ability to present God's salvation story with exceptional clarity in a way that convicts people of their need for Christ. It is our guess that Billy Graham has the gift of evangelism.

Disposition Gifts—The Power to Serve

- *Giving:* This gift has nothing to do with the amount of money you give. It involves unusual sensitivity to identifying special needs, along with overwhelming generosity with whatever means God has given to you.

- *Mercy:* All of us should be sensitive to the needs of other people; we should be available to comfort them in their times of trouble and discouragement. But most of us are oblivious to these circumstances, or we don't desire to do it. A person with the gift of mercy has both the attitude and action.

- *Serving:* It may take many forms, but people with this spiritual gift have sensitivity for knowing how they can be of help to other people. More important than just knowing what to do, their gift empowers them to spring into action and get the job done. Usually, these acts of service are very practical.

• *Administration:* Being in a position of leadership doesn't necessarily mean that you have the gift of administration, but it sure would help. This gift equips a person with good judgment and people skills for leadership in the church.

What Do I Do with It?

Bible scholars have spent considerable time and brainpower trying to analyze and compare these passages. No one has a complete understanding of these passages, but several observations have been made:

1. While all of these passages make reference to gifts of the Holy Spirit, their basic orientation is different. The verses from Ephesians suggest that these are roles within the church. The Romans and 1 Peter passages actually catalog several basic functions that are performed within the church. And the 1 Corinthians verses seem to be a list of special abilities. Because they have slightly different meanings in mind, no one should bust a gut trying to reduce

the passages into a single, unified concept or definition of spiritual gifts.

2. It is not clear when a person receives a spiritual gift. The predominant view is that a spiritual gift is received when a person becomes a Christian. If someone has multiple spiritual gifts, one may be given at the time of salvation, and another gift may be given later in time.

3. Some gifts, such as faith and service, are qualities that every believer is required to have. In such cases, the spiritual gifts of faith and service, for example, may be unusually strong capabilities in those areas.

Spiritual Gifts Given to Some	Commands Given to All
Service	Serve one another (Galatians 5:13).
Encouragement	Encourage one another (Hebrews 10:25).
Giving	Give generously (2 Corinthians 9:7).
Teaching	Tell others about Jesus (Matthew 28:19).
Mercy	Be kind (Ephesians 4:32).
Faith	Walk by faith (2 Corinthians 5:7).
Evangelism	Be a witness to others (Acts 1:8).

You can't avoid your responsibilities as a Christian simply by saying, "Hey, that's not my gift."

4. Since none of the four lists includes all of the gifts found in the other lists, it is possible that collectively they do not exhaust all gifts of the Spirit. Individually and collectively, they might be representative (rather than exhaustive) of the type of supernatural empowerment that God gives to believers.

When you get to the bottom line of spiritual gifts, there are only two things that you should do:

1. Find out what your spiritual gift is; and

2. Start using it.

This happens only as you get involved in ministry to other people. Remember, a spiritual gift is given to you by the Holy Spirit for the purpose of helping others. You won't discover your spiritual gift, or be able to use it, if you keep to yourself and have no contact with other people. Get involved in some of the ministries of your church. Volunteer to help out with some projects. Before long, you (and the people you are working with) may recognize that you have a special sensitivity or ability. That may be evidence of your spiritual gift.

WHAT THE SPIRITUAL GIFTS LOOK LIKE IN ACTION

Imagine that several people from your church are in a meeting. It has been going for a long while, and someone asks a young boy to bring a pitcher of water and some glasses into the room. The boy trips, and the pitcher of water spills all over the table. The spiritual gifts of each person in the room prompt them into immediate action:

- The person with the gift of service grabs a towel and starts mopping up the water.

- The person with the gift of mercy begins to comfort the distraught boy.

- The person with the gift of teaching shows the boy how to hold the pitcher so it won't spill next time.

- The person with the gift of encouragement tells the boy that he'll do better next time.

- And the person with the gift of leadership asks, "Who put this boy in charge of carrying the water?"

Okay, we are being a bit sarcastic, but you get the idea.

In the Dig Deeper section at the end of this chapter are the titles of some books that will give you helpful information for ways to discover your spiritual gift.

No one will benefit from your spiritual gift if you keep it under wraps. Find it and use it, and begin to experience the supernatural power of the Holy Spirit in your life.

"What's That Again?"

1. Jesus promised that His followers would have supernatural power. That power is a "spiritual gift" from the Holy Spirit.

2. Spiritual gifts are special abilities and sensitivities that benefit the Christian community. The Holy Spirit gives these gifts to believers as He chooses.

3. Every believer has at least one spiritual gift.

4. Spiritual gifts are not connected with a particular place or position in the church.

5. As with any gift, you should be anxious to find out what your spiritual gift is, and you should begin to use it. That will only happen as you get involved in ministry to other people.

Dig Deeper

We know that you'll find further study about the dynamic power of the Holy Spirit to be interesting, but it is also imperative. Here are three books you can find at a Christian bookstore or at a used bookshop that we heartily recommend:

Operating in the Power of the Holy Spirit by Larry Keefauver isn't really a book. It is set up as a 30-day devotional guide. You can go through it by yourself or in a group.

Ronald E. Baxter does an excellent job of defining and classifying the spiritual gifts in his book *Gifts of the Spirit*.

Pastor Charles Stanley has a study guide called *Ministering Through Spiritual Gifts* that may help you discover and use your spiritual gift.

There seems to be more confusion about the gift of praying in the Spirit than any other spiritual gift. *The Charismatic Gift of Tongues,* also by Ronald E. Baxter, gives an objective approach to this subject.

Moving On

This book is finished, but your adventure with the Holy Spirit may just be starting. The Holy Spirit is ready, willing, and able to create a vibrant, exciting, and dynamic spiritual life within you. But the Holy Spirit is a perfect gentleman, so He won't force Himself on you. He'll wait until you are ready to let Him take leadership in your life.

Paul said to "let the Holy Spirit fill and control you" (Ephesians 5:18). That verse isn't just a suggestion; it is a command. In its context, the verse suggests that the filling of the Holy Spirit is not a one-time event; it is an ongoing action that you should start now and keeping working at. We all need to work harder at relinquishing control of our lives to the Holy Spirit. As that happens, our lives will reflect the fruit of the Spirit, and we will be more effective at using the spiritual gifts that the Holy Spirit has given to us. It is all a matter of being filled by the Spirit instead of being filled with ourselves.

Remember: The filling of the Holy Spirit doesn't involve you getting more out of the Holy Spirit. Rather, it is a matter of the Holy Spirit getting more of you.

About the Authors

Bruce Bickel is a lawyer, but he didn't start out that bad. After college, he considered the noble profession of a stand-up comic, but he had to abandon that dream because he is not very funny. As a lawyer, he makes people laugh (but it is not on purpose).

Stan Jantz is a retail-marketing consultant. From the time he was a little kid, Stan's family owned a chain of Christian bookstores, so he feels very comfortable behind the counter.

Bruce and Stan spend their free time as "cultural observers" (they made that term up). They watch how God applies to real life. Together they have written more than 25 books.

Other Books by the Guys

Bruce & Stan Search for the Meaning of Life
Bruce & Stan's® Guide to the Bible
Bruce & Stan's® Guide to Bible Prophecy
Bruce & Stan's® Guide to God
Bruce & Stan's® Guide to How It All Began
Bruce & Stan's® Pocket Guide to Finding God's Will
Bruce & Stan's® Pocket Guide to Knowing Jesus
Bruce & Stan's® Pocket Guide to Sharing Your Faith
Bruce & Stan's® Pocket Guide to Studying the Bible
Bruce & Stan's® Pocket Guide to Prayer
God Is in the Small Stuff (and It All Matters)
Keeping God in the Small Stuff
Real Life Has No Expiration Date

Bruce and Stan would enjoy hearing from you. (If you've got something nice to say, then don't hold back. If you have a criticism, then be gentle.) The best way to contact them is:

E-mail: **guide@bruceandstan.com**
Snail Mail: Bruce & Stan
P.O. Box 25565, Fresno, CA 93729-5565

You can learn more than you ever wanted to know about Bruce and Stan by visiting their Web site: **www.bruceandstan.com**